Swamp Wallaby™
and the
Big Wave

Swamp Wallaby™ and the Big Wave

Written by
Tracey West and John Schneider

Created and Illustrated by
John Schneider

Designed by Jesse Sanchez

RED SKY PRESENTS

Published by
RED SKY PRESENTS

141 E. 72nd Street, 12th Floor
New York, NY 10021
http://redskypresents.com/
redskypresents@gmail.com

For Children.

ISBN: 978-1-941015-23-0

Swamp Wallaby #1: The Big Wave

Chapter One:
The Challenge

"Bonza!" yelled Swamp Wallaby. "Woo hoo! All right! Yee ha!"

Swamp was balancing on an old log.

"Killer wave," he told his friend Rocksy. "What a rip snorter! A real bottler!"

"I do not understand a word you are saying," Rocksy said.

Swamp flipped up his sunglasses. "Come on, Rocks. That means I just rode an awesome wave."

Rocksy looked down. Swamp's surfboard was on top of a rock, not a wave. The rock stuck out of a small puddle.

"But Swamp," she said. "You are surfing in a puddle."

Swamp shrugged. "Sure. But I am a surfer. A surfer needs to surf."

Swamp, Rocksy, and Swamp's family lived in Australia, in a place called the Outback. The ground was red, dusty and scattered with tufts of dry grass. The only wave in sight was Wave Rock. It was not made of water. The giant rock looked like a big ocean wave.

Swamp lived there because it reminded him of the ocean. That was a little strange, because a wallaby is not an ocean animal. Wallabies are furry. They have long tails. Their ears are pointy. They have strong back legs. They look like kangaroos but they are much smaller.

They are also not surfers. Well, most of them are not.

"A surfer also needs waves," Rocksy pointed out. "When are you going to make a trip to the ocean?"

Beep! Beep!

Just then, an emu drove by in a kombi van. Another emu was riding in the open back of the van. She tossed a piece of paper at Swamp. The paper landed on his nose.

"Wow, Rocksy, check this out!" he said.

"This is perfect! We can form an extreme team and join the challenge."

Rocksy grinned. "I like the sound of that. I've

been hanging around here for too long. But how will we find the Secret Beach? And what's a Giant Fist?"

Swamp climbed off the log. "I know who might be able to help us. Cousin Didj!"

Are you ready for the
EXTREME Outback Challenge?

\# Then form an **EXTREME** team!

\# There will be 12 **EXTREME** challenges in all.

\# The first **EXTREME** team to complete all 12 will win an **EXTREME** prize.

\# First challenge: find the Secret Beach and surf the Giant Fist.

Chapter Two: Cousin Didj

Swamp and Rocksy headed for Didj's cave. As they got closer they could hear a low, humming sound.

"Didj must be playing his didgeridoo," Swamp guessed.

The music got louder when they got inside the dark cave. Glow worm threads dangled from the ceiling. Cave beetles skittered around the cave. Centipedes with lots of legs crawled everywhere.

"Creepy crawly bugs sure love Didj's music," Rocksy said.

They found Swamp's cousin in the middle of the cave. Didj was blowing into his didgeridoo - a long, hollow branch that had been eaten out by termites. It was decorated with white dots and lines. He stopped playing when he saw Swamp and Rocksy.

"Swamp! Rocksy! What brings you to my cozy cave?" he asked.

Swamp showed him the flyer. "The EXTREME Outback Challenge," he said. "We need you on our team. You used to be a surfer. Do you know where the Secret Beach is?"

"And do you know about the Giant Fist?" asked Rocksy.

Didj shuddered. "Yes and yes. But I will never tell you where the Secret Beach is. I have seen the Giant Fist with my own eyes."

"You have?" Swamp asked.

Didj nodded. "Yes. The Giant Fist is a really big wave. It's a monster. It eats surfboards like they are candy. It shaves the fur off wallabies until they are as bald as soccer balls."

"That sounds intense," said Rocksy.

"It sure is," said Didj. "That's why I can't tell you where it is."

"But Didj, it's the EXTREME Outback Challenge!" Swamp said. "I was riding my log at Wave Rock. And then the flyer fell right on my nose. Don't you see? I was born to do this. If you don't tell me where the Secret Beach is, I will find it on my own."

Didj was quiet for a minute. "All right," he said. "I think I can find it again. But I will have to go with you."

"Welcome to the team!" Rocksy said.

"We can take my kombi van," added Swamp.

"This calls for a song," Didj said. He blew into his didgeridoo . . .

. . . and a big, long snake popped out the other end.

"Aaaaaaaaah!" screamed Swamp and Rocksy.

Chapter Three: Road Trip!

"That's just Gizmo," said Didj. "He's my friend."

Gizmo slid out of the didgeridoo. Swamp took a step back.

"I would rather ride the Giant Fist than be friends with a snake," he said.

"Well, Gizmo is coming with us," said Didj.

"Does he have to?" asked Swamp.

"Chill out, man," said Didj. "Gizmo is cool. Come on, Gizmo."

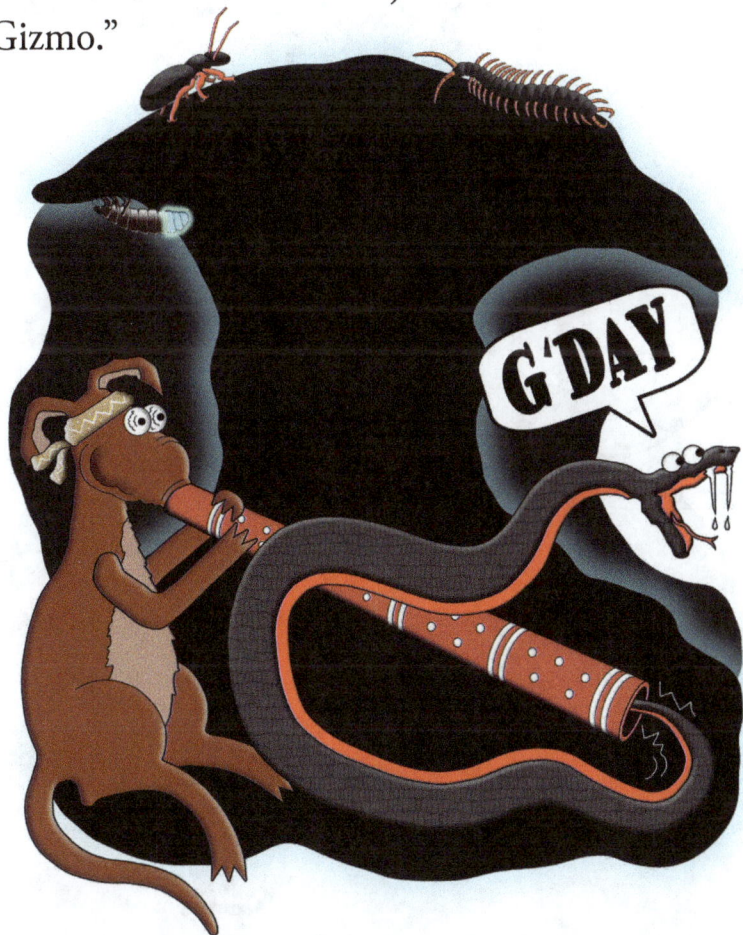

On the way to Swamp's van, a wheelchair whizzed past them. Inside was an old, gray wallaby with a white beard. Two smaller wallabies were pushing the chair. "- Super speed Swampah!" the smaller wallabies yelled.

"Bilby! Jilby! Stop pushing Swampah!" Swamp scolded.

Bilby and Jilby were twins, and Swamp's little

When I was a kid, I was happy playing with a stick!

brother and sister. Swampah was their grandfather. Bilby and Jilby quickly stopped. Swampah swung the chair around.

"It's okay, Swamp!" he said. "We were having fun."

Then Bilby and Jilby saw Gizmo crawling on the ground. They weren't scared at all.

"Jump rope!" they yelled at once. Jilby handed Gizmo's tail to Swampah. Bilby grabbed Gizmo's head. Swampah and Bilby swung the snake like a jump rope, and Jilby jumped over it.

"Well, have fun," Swamp said. "We're going on a road trip. I'm not sure when we'll be back."

Swampah dropped Gizmo's tail. "Now hold on there! A road trip? Where to?"

"We're going to enter the EXTREME Outback Challenge," Swamp said. "First we have to

surf the Giant Fist."

Swampah got a worried look on his face. "Listen here, young fella. I can't let you do that. It's too dangerous."

"That's what I told him," said Didj. "But he's going to do it no matter what."

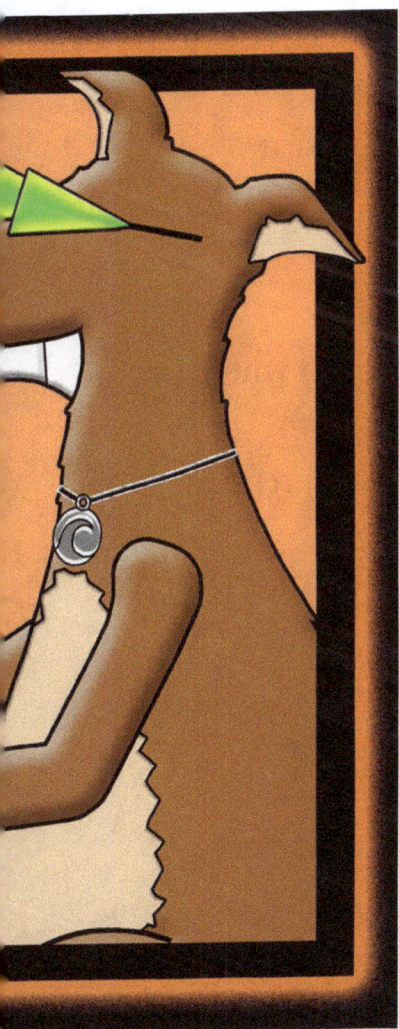

Swamp nodded. "Nothing EXTREME ever happens out here. I need a challenge. Something new."

Swampah sighed. "In that case, I won't stop you."

Swamp smiled. "Thanks!"

"We'll all go!" said Swampah. "Bilby, Jilby, we're going on a road trip!"

"Road trip!" the twins cheered.

Swamp thought about being stuck in the van with the twins for days and days.

"Oh nooooo!" he groaned.

Chapter Four: Lost

"Jump in!" called out Rocksy as the wallabies bounced into the kombi van. The big, green, van was splattered with red Outback dust. There was plenty of room inside for all of the wallabies.

Swamp jumped into the driver's seat.

"Shotgun!" Rocksy called out, and took the seat next to Swamp.

"Not fair!" wailed Bilby and Jilby.

Swamp revved up the engine. "So where to, Didj?" he asked.

"Well, I'm not exactly sure," Didj replied. "For now, head south and east.

"Will do!" said Swamp. "Let the EXTREME road trip begin!"

"Let's sing a road song," Jilby suggested, as the van pulled onto the road.

"Yeah!" agreed Bilby.

Then the twins began to sing.

"Give me a home among the gum trees,
with lots of sun please,
a wave or two,
a kangaroo,
a kombi for the trip,
a surfboard on the rack,
and Swampah in the back!"

Swamp made a face. "Can you keep it down, please?" he asked. But Bilby and Jilby kept singing.

Swamp turned to Rocksy. "I can't believe we have to drag them along," he said, but Rocksy was already asleep.

He looked in the mirror. Didj and Swampah were asleep too. Swamp sighed.

"How can they sleep through that racket?" he wondered.

So Swamp drove through the red sands of the Outback. And drove . . . and drove . . .

Then he realized he wasn't on a road anymore. Red desert sand stretched out all around him. The bleached bones of Outback critters gleamed in the sand.

"Uh-oh," said Swamp.

Rocksy opened her eyes. "Are we there yet?"

"I don't think so," Swamp said. "I think we're lost. That's what the sign says, anyway."

Swampah's eyes opened. "Rubbish! It says we are *probably* lost. Swamp, I think you need a break. If you drive when you're tired we'll end up like those bones!"

OUTBACK
YOU'RE PROBABLY LOST

PAINT

That woke up Didj. "Lost? In the middle of Whoop-Whoop? That's a worry, mate!"

"I'll take over the wheel," Rocksy offered. "Get some sleep, Swamp."

Bilby and Jilby stopped singing. They had been twisting Gizmo into different shapes, now their eyes bulged out of the window staring at death.

water?

"Sounds good," said Swamp, and he closed his eyes.

Rocksy looked up at the sun in the sky. "South and east. That should get us back to the road."

She steered the van over the bumpy ground. The dusty road was full of rocks and hills.

Bump! The van hit a big bump. Rocksy's sunglasses bounced on her nose.

Bump! The steering wheel fell right into Rocksy's lap.

"Uh-oh," said Rocksy. She quickly picked up the wheel.

Bump! Rocksy's sunglasses flew right off her face! The sun hit her eyes, and she couldn't see. Startled, she tossed the steering wheel into the air. It fell out the window.

"Help!" Rocksy cried. She couldn't see anything in the bright sun. She couldn't steer the van. It was a crash waiting to happen!

Swamp was fast asleep next to her. Didj and Swampah were snoring, too.

Then Rocksy felt something slither under her paws. She looked down. Gizmo had wrapped himself around the steering pole.

"Hang on tight," he told Rocksy.

Rocksy gasped. "You can talk?"

25

"I can do a lot of thingsss," said Gizmo. "Now quick! Sssteer right!"

Rocksy gripped Gizmo and steered the van right.

"Now left!" said Gizmo.

Rocksy steered right.

"Now left! Now right! Fassster! Fassster! Now right again! Now left!"

"This is crazy!" yelled Rocksy.

"Yes, but we're missing all the bumpsss," said Gizmo.

Bump!

"Well, almost all the bumpsss," Gizmo said.

Rocksy slammed on the brakes. Swamp, Didj, and Swampah all woke up.

"Enough!" she said. "I need to find the real steering wheel."

"You mean that steering wheel?" Bilby asked, pointing out the window.

Rocksy looked out the window. There was the steering wheel—and her sunglasses. "We must have been driving in circles."

"See? I found them for you," said Gizmo.

Didj climbed out of the van and got the steering wheel and the sunglasses. Rocksy put her sunglasses back on and bolted the steering wheel back into place.

"Back to the bumpy road," she said with a sigh.

Chapter Five: Duck!

Didj hopped up to the front. "I'll give it a go, Rocks. You've just got to chill. Be one with the road."

"Good luck," Rocksy said.

Didj started up the van. "Smooth and easy," he said.

Soon they were back on the main road.

"So where are we now?" Swamp asked.

"I'm not sure," replied Didj. "But all roads lead somewhere, right?"

"So we're still lost," said Rocksy.

"I'm hungry!" wailed Jilby.

"I'm tired!" wailed Bilby.

"And I'm hungry and tired!" wailed Swampah.

Swamp looked out the window. The sun was setting. The sky was starting to turn dark blue.

"Let's find a place to camp for the night," he said.

So the wallabies set up their sleeping bags under the stars. Rocksy started a campfire and Swamp cooked up some damper bread baked in the hot coals. Then he added potatoes wrapped in foil. (Because all wallabies are vegetarians.) They soon fell asleep and woke up with the sunrise.

"So Didj, can you get us back on the right road today?" Swamp asked, as they ate their oat porridge the next morning.

"I can't wait to find this wave. I was born to surf the Giant Fist."

"Yes, we know," said Rocksy.

Didj shrugged. "I'm not sure. We'll just go where the road takes us. We'll get there sooner or later."

"Sooner would be better," Swamp said.

"Then let's get back in the van," said Rocksy, getting up and stretching. They hopped back into the green van. Swamp took the wheel.

Didj stuck his didgeridoo out the back window and played a song.

They didn't get far when Bilby and Jilby cried out, "Look! Out the window!"

A big red kangaroo was hopping along next to the van. He smiled at Swamp.

"G'day, mates!" he said cheerfully. "Name's Boomeroo. What are you doing here in these parts?"

"We want to enter the EXTREME Outback Challenge. We're trying to find the Secret Beach," replied Swamp. "But we're kind of lost."

"Do you know how we can get to the coast?" Rocksy asked.

"Follow me!" said Boomeroo. "I'll show you the way. And you can meet some of my best mates. They're just down the road. But watch your heads!"

"What did he mean by that?" Rocksy wondered, but Boomeroo had already started hopping away.

"Thanks!" Swamp called after him, as he followed the kangaroo. Suddenly, Rocksy frowned.

"What's up ahead? A flock of birds?" she asked.

The air in front of them was filled with flying things. But they didn't look like birds to Swamp.

One came flying closer . . . and flew right

through the open window!

"Boomerang!" yelled Rocksy, ducking.

Boomeroo zoomed ahead and caught up to his kangaroo friends. They tossed even more boomerangs into the air. Boomeroo whacked one of his mates on the nose with his boomerang and sent them all flying backwards. The wallabies thought it was the goofiest thing they had ever seen.

Some of the boomerangs that were still in the air whipped around the van.

"Duck!" yelled Swamp, as more boomerangs flew

through the open back window. One of them knocked over Didj! Another one knocked over Swampah! The wallabies screamed and ducked as the boomerangs swirled around them.

Swamp had to keep his eyes on the road. He tried to steer through all the flying boomerangs. The van swerved left, then right, then left, then right.

"This is worse than the bumpy road!" yelled Rocksy.

Then the road came to a fork. Boomeroo pointed to the left side.

"You're still hundreds of miles away, but that'll get you to the coast, mates!" he called out. "It was good bumping into you! See ya!"

"You too!" Swamp called back, as another boomerang whizzed past his nose. He quickly swerved to the left, and the wallabies left the boomerang-loving kangaroos behind them.

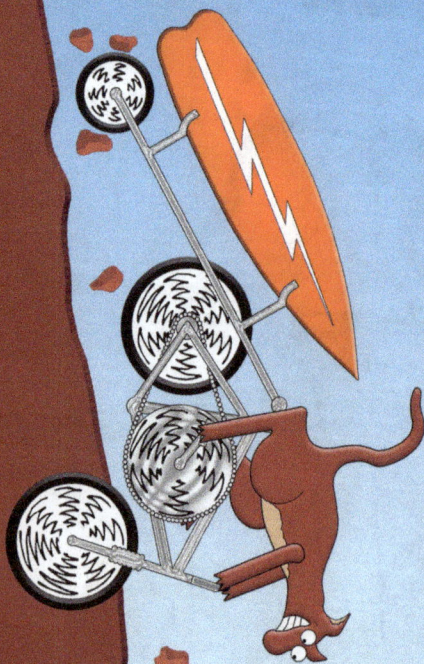

Chapter Six: Follow That Surfer!

"I hope that Boomeroo fellow steered us right," said Swamp. They had been driving for hours, and were still in the Outback.

"Maybe he has," said Rocksy, pointing. "Look up ahead. Is that a surfboard?"

In front of them, a wallaby was riding a mountain bike and pulling a trailer behind it. Strapped to the trailer was an orange surfboard!

"We must be close to the coast," said Swamp, excited. "Maybe we're even close to the Giant Fist!"

"Follow him!" Rocksy said.

The wallaby soon took a turn off the main road. Swamp followed him down a steep cliff.

"Whoa! This is not very chill!" cried Didj.

Swamp looked at the scene in front of him. "Check this place out!"

The cliff led to a rocky plain. Up ahead, they could see two huge buffaloes.

"This does not look like the coast," said Rocksy.

Swamp stopped the van. "This is very strange," he said. "Let's check it out."

The wallabies climbed out of the van. A bunch of other wallabies carrying surfboards were walking past one of the buffaloes. He was pulling a big rock up to the top of a cliff.

Swamp and the others hopped up to get a closer look. The other buffalo was standing at the edge of a deep gorge. Swamp looked down. There was water in the bottom of the gorge.

"Ready for the next wave!" called out a red kangaroo. Three wallabies with surfboards jumped onto a big rock. The kangaroo yelled out a command to the buffalo. The huge beast grunted and pushed the rock over the edge and into the gorge!

Splash! The rock made a big wave when it hit the water. The surfers jumped off the rock and rode the wave.

"They're surfing in a billabong," said Swamp, amazed.

"What's a billabong?" asked Bilby and Jilby.

"It's a pond," said Swamp. "This one is in the middle of nowhere."

The kangaroo hopped over to them. He smiled and held out his paw.

"I'm Maliroo," he said. "Welcome to the Outback School of Surfing!"

"Surfing in the Outback!" said Swamp. "That's awesome."

"I had to find a way to surf out here," said Maliroo. "I've got surfing in my bones."

"Me too!" Swamp said...

"Excuse me," said Rocksy. "But you remind me of someone. Do you know a kangaroo named Boomeroo?"

"Why, that's my cousin!" said Maliroo.

MALIROO'S OUTBACK SCHOOL OF SURFING

BEGINNERS FREE

Chapter Seven: The Outback School of Surfing

"Any friend of Boomeroo's is a friend of mine. How would you and your family like some free lessons?"

"Yay! Surfing!" yelled Bilby and Jilby.

"Not you two," said Swamp, looking at the deep drop into the pond. "You're too little."

"Not fair!" the twins complained.

"No problem," said Maliroo.

"We can start with balancing lessons on land. Everyone can do that. Unless any of you are pros?"

"Well, I used to surf a lot, but I'm a little rusty," said Didj.

"And I practice every day! said Swamp. He picked up one of Maliroo's surfboards and stood it on its end. Then he jumped up onto the end and balanced perfectly on one foot!

"Beauty!" said Maliroo. "Maybe you can help me with the others, then."

So the wallabies had a fun time practicing surfing on land. Swamp held up a surfboard so Rocksy could balance on top of it.

Bilby and Jilby balanced on the horns of the big buffalo. Didj balanced on Gizmo. Even Swampah practiced. He balanced a surfboard on top of his cane. Then he balanced his wheelchair on top of the surfboard! As fun as it was, Swamp was itching to ride a real wave.

"Can I give the billabong a try?" he asked Maliroo.

"You bet!" cried Maliroo. "Grab your board and hop on that rock."

Swamp jumped on the rock. His tail twitched with excitement.

"Time for another wave!" yelled Maliroo, and he tapped the buffalo on the back.

"Let's go Biff!"

The buffalo pushed. The rock dropped. Swamp's heart beat fast as he fell down into the pond.

"Now jump!" Maliroo called out.

Swamp gripped his board. He jumped off the rock just before it hit the water.

"Paddle!"

Swamp got on his belly and paddled in the water. *Splash!*

The rock hit the pond. Swamp could feel the wave rising up behind him.

"On your board!" yelled Maliroo.

Swamp quickly stood up. He was balancing! He was riding on the wave! And then . . .

. . . the wave quickly died. Swamp tumbled into the pond.

"Bonza!" he yelled, splashing to the shore.

"You gotta try it, Rocksy! It's awesome!"

Maliroo yelled to the other buffalo. "Another rock please, Buff!"

Swamp had the best evening ever. He, Rocksy, Swampah and Didj rode wave after wave in the billabong."

They're the best waves we can make out here," Maliroo said. "But it's a good way to learn."

"Soon I'll be riding the Giant Fist," Swamp told him. "The biggest wave of all."

Maliroo's eyes got big. "Really, mate? That's mighty dangerous."

"It's for the EXTREME Outback Challenge," Swamp told him.

"Good on ya, then, mate!" Maliroo said.

Chapter Eight: Swamp's Dream

That night, as the wallabies slept under the stars, Swamp dreamed of the ocean. As he stood on the shore, a big wave formed in the water. It looked like a monster with teeth as white as ocean foam.

In his dream, Swamp saw two surfers paddling in front of the wave. Two wallabies.

It was his mom and dad! They disappeared when Swamp was a kid. But he still remembered them. He always thought about them.

The monster wave got bigger and bigger. His parents stood up on their surfboards. Then the monster wave crashed over them . . .

"Mom! Dad!" Swamp yelled. He woke up from his dream. He was covered in sweat.

Swampah was sitting in his wheelchair, looking down on Swamp. He looked Swamp right in the eyes.

"Swamp, we need to talk," he said.

47

Swamp dragged himself out of his sleeping bag and sat on a rock next to Swampah.

"Swamp, did you just dream about a monster wave?" he asked.

Swamp nodded.

"I had the same dream," Swampah said. He was quiet for a moment. Then he asked, "Swamp, do you remember your mom and dad?"

"I do," Swamp said. "But not much. I remember that once they took Didj and me on vacation to the ocean when we were little joeys. They were surfing. We watched them ride their surfboards on the waves. That's why I have been learning how to surf all these years."

"They loved to surf," Swampah said. Tears started to fill his eyes. "They went to the ocean every summer. Your mother would surf the waves until her fur was soaked through. And your father was so proud of his surfboard. He would rub it with wax every morning before he hit the waves."

Swamp nodded. "I think I remember it smelled nice...like coconuts." He closed his eyes, remembering.

"But I still don't know why they disappeared. Or why we never went to the ocean again after they were gone."

Swampah sighed. "They were surfing, Swamp. I didn't see it. I was watching you and your little brother and sister. They were just babies then. But your

48

parents went on a weekend surfing trip with your Uncle Bluey, Didj's dad."

Swamp's eyes got wide. "What happened?"

"Bluey said it was a wave . . . a monster wave," Swampah said. "It washed over them . . . and then he never saw them again. Nobody has. They've been lost ever since. We didn't tell you how it happened, well, because . . . I'm not sure. But I guess you knew, deep down."

Swamp looked up at the stars, sad. No wonder Swampah didn't want him to surf the Giant Fist. He didn't want to lose Swamp, too.

"Swamp, you okay?"

Didj had woken up. He hopped over to Swamp. Before Swamp could answer, Didj gasped and pointed up to the sky.

"Of course!" he cried. "The Southern Cross!"

Didj was pointing to five stars in the sky—four bright ones, and one dim one in between them all. If you drew a line connecting the two stars from the east and west, and another line connecting the two stars from the north and south, you would make a cross. Swamp knew that's how the constellation got its name.

"What about it?" Swamp asked.

"That's what we need to follow!" Didj said. "I remember now. If we follow the Southern Cross we'll get to the Secret Beach."

Swamp shook his head. "Forget about it, Didj. We're done."

"What do you mean, dude?" his cousin asked.

"I mean, this road trip is over," said Swamp.

"I am not riding the Giant Fist. Tomorrow morning, we're going home!"

Chapter Nine: Rescue!

Swamp went back to sleep. Then some sounds drifted into his sleeping brain . . .

"Help! Help!"

Swamp woke right up. That was Jilby's voice. And it was coming from the billabong!

Swamp hopped past Rocksy, his family, the surfers, and Maliroo, who were all asleep. He raced to the edge of the billabong and jumped in

Splash! He swam over to Jilby, who was next to one of the big rocks in the pond.

"Bilby's trapped!" Jilby cried. "His tail's caught under the rock!"

Swamp took a deep breath. He dove underwater and swam as fast as he could go. He swam down, down to the bottom of the pond.

He saw Bilby, with his cheeks puffed out with air, yanking on his tail. It was stuck under the rock! Swamp swam to him and pulled at the rock with all his might. He felt stronger than he ever had before. The rock moved a teeny, tiny bit—just enough to free Bilby's tail. Then Swamp grabbed his little brother and swam back up to the surface as fast as he could. Swamp gasped for air. Bilby opened his eyes and took a deep breath. He was all right!

Then Swamp heard clapping and cheering.
He looked up. Rocksy, Swampah, and Didj were
standing around the pond.

"I think he's fine," Swamp said, hopping up to the

shore. Rocksy draped Bilby in a towel. The little
wallaby looked soaked and scared. Jilby bumped noses
with Bilby.

"I'm glad you little critters are okay," Swampah
said. "But now tell me, what were you two doing

in the billabong? You know you weren't supposed to go there."

Jilby looked down. "Well, we didn't think it was fair that we couldn't go surfing," she said.

"So we woke up really early and borrowed some

surfboards. I jumped on the rock, and Bilby tapped the buffalo. The buffalo pushed the rock, but Bilby slipped and didn't get on the rock on time. We're really sorry."

"Yeah, we're really s-s-sorry," Bilby said with a shiver.

"That was very dangerous," Swampah said. "You are lucky that Swamp saved you in time."

"Which is exactly why we're heading home this morning," said Swamp. "And believe me, we'll keep a close eye on you two the whole way home."

"I can help," Gizmo said, wrapping himself around Bilby's ankle.

"Keeping an eye on the twins is a good idea," Swampah agreed. "But we are not going home."

Swamp was confused. "What?"

"You were very brave, Swamp," Swampah said. "You kept calm under pressure. You held your breath for a long time. And you swim and surf like a real pro."

Rocksy nodded, "I agree."

"You have what it takes to ride the Giant Fist," Swampah said.

"Are you sure?" Swamp asked.

Swampah smiled. "I can feel it in my old wallaby bones."

Didj looked up at the early morning sky. He could still see the faint stars of the Southern Cross.

"I can get us there," he said. "Swamp, are you sure?"

Swamp looked at Swampah's proud face.

"To the van!" Swamp cried.

The wallabies yelled out a loud goodbye and a big thank you to Maliroo and the surfers as they took off down the road.

Chapter Ten:
The Ocean at Last!

Following the sun by day and the Southern Cross by night, the wallabies drove for days. Then finally reached the Great Australian Bight—the large, carved coast in the southern part of Australia.

The smooth road snaked along the coast. The air smelled of salt. On one side, a rocky cliff rose up next to them, dotted with bushy green trees. On the other side was the beautiful green-blue ocean.

Bilby and Jilby couldn't stop looking out the window. They had never seen the ocean before.

"It's so big!" said Jilby.

"And the waves never stop moving!" Bilby said.

"We are getting closer," said Didj. "The Secret Beach is at the end of this road. That's where we'll find the Giant Fist."

Swamp felt the ends of his fur tingle. It was really happening! He was going to ride the Giant Fist.

"Hey, pull into that surf shop up ahead," Swampah said.

Everyone was glad to have a break. Bilby and

Jilby grabbed two boogie boards and hopped on them, pretending to ride the waves. Rocksy and Didj looked at sunhats. Then Jilby and Bilby ran to the other side of the shop and tried out sunscreen with Gizmo.

"I have to keep my scalesss sssafe," he said.

Swamp got lost looking at all the surfing gear. His heart pounded with excitement. There were long-boards and thrusters and bodyboards and funboards and foamboards and boards with graphics. Swamp wanted to try them all.

Swampah seemed to disappear for a while. Then he rolled into the store.

"Come on, we've got to hook up the trailer!" he called out.

"The trailer?" Swamp wondered.

The wallabies followed Swampah outside. Brand new surfboards were sticking out of the windows of the van. Behind the van was a trailer with a shiny yellow and black wave bike on it.

"Swampah, what's all this?" Swamp asked.

"I have some money put aside from all the surfing competitions I won," he said.

Everyone stared at him, speechless.

"Well, why do you think everyone in our family is so good at surfing?" he asked. "You little critters all got it from me!"

"But what's the wave bike for?" Rocksy asked.

"The biggest waves are so fast that you need a fast wave bike to catch up to them," Swampah explained. "The wave bike tows the surfer into the wave, and the rider lets go when it's time to ride the wave."

Didj nodded. "I've done that before. I can pull

you, Swamp."

"Thanks, Didj," he said, and his fur started to tingle again. Things were getting real.

Swampah noticed the look on his face. "You okay, Swamp?" he asked.

"I think so," Swamp said. "Just a little nervous."

"Well, you don't have to be nervous for long," said Didj. "We're lucky. The weather is perfect for surfing. In a few hours, you'll be riding the Giant Fist!"

Chapter Eleven:
Team Whalloping Wallabies!

Didj took over driving. After about an hour he turned off the main road. A dirt road took them through old gum trees growing from sandy soil.

Then the road opened up to a small, deserted beach. In the middle of the sand was a big, red canopy tent. It said, "EXTREME Outback Challenge" on the sides. Next to it, a rescue helicopter was parked.

They hopped out of the van and went up to the tent. An emu was sitting behind a table.

"G'day, mates!" she said cheerfully. "Welcome to the EXTREME Outback Challenge. Looks like you found the Secret Beach."

"Are we the first ones here?" Swamp asked.

"A team of wombats beat you," the emu answered. "But they didn't have much luck with the Giant Fist. We needed to rescue them."

She nodded to a corner
of the tent. Two wombats were huddled in
the corner, wrapped in towels.

"Well, I'm feeling lucky today," said Swamp.

The emu picked up a clipboard. "Let's get you
entered. What's your team name?"

Swamp looked at Rocksy and his family.
He hadn't thought of that before.

"How about,
Team Whalloping
Wallabies?"
Rocksy suggested.

"Perfect!"
said Swamp.

The emu wrote
that down. "Okay, then.
Good luck!"

They left the tent
and walked down
to the water.

A wave as tall as a house rose up in the distance. The wall of water zoomed toward the shore.

"Wow! Was that the Giant Fist?" asked Jilby.

"That was just a big wave," Didj said. "But not the Giant Fist. When the Giant Fist comes you'll know it."

Rocksy gave Swamp a worried look.

"Are you sure about this, Swamp?" she asked.

"Sure as I'll ever be," Swamp said. "But I'd like to get some practice in first."

"Good idea!" Swampah agreed. He wheeled his chair onto a surfboard. "I've always wanted to surf this old wheelchair on a longboard!"

Swamp got into the ocean. Swampah was ready...waiting on the sand...hoping he would catch the same wave as Swamp.

Swamp paddled out into the water. He felt the ocean move under him. The wave came behind him, and he stood on his board. He kept his balance as he rode the wave into the shore.

"Bonza!" he yelled.

"Nice job, Swamp!" Rocksy yelled.

Then Bilby and Jilby started hopping up and down.

"Look! Look!"

Far out in the ocean, a massive wave was forming. As it moved closer, they all could see how really huge it was.

Didj pushed the wave bike into the water. "It's a good practice wave Swamp. We've got to ride this one first. The Giant Fist is a monster wave but it is much bigger and will be behind this one," he explained. "Quick, hook up!"

Swamp grabbed onto the ski rope attached to the wave bike. Didj turned on the motor and sped out to catch up to the wave.

Swamp's paws tightened on the ski rope. He knew that as soon as the wave bike reached the same speed as the wave, he would let go.

Suddenly, the huge wave was looming over them. The white foam on top of the wave took shape and it also had two big watery claws!

"It's a monster wave!" Swamp yelled, and his heart started to beat faster.

One of its massive claws reached out and grabbed the wave bike. The other one grabbed Swamp's surfboard. Swamp was connected to it with a tail strap, and the big wave dangled him over the water.

"Help!" screamed Swamp and Didj.

Swamp looked down. Thanks to the tail strap, he was only a few feet above the water. If the wave dropped him, he'd be okay.

But the wave dangled Didj high above the water. If the wave tossed Didj . . . Swamp didn't want to think about it.

Then a loud noise filled the air, a noise louder than the roaring of the wave. Swamp looked up.

It was the rescue helicopter—and Swampah was flying it! He flew toward Didj. The helicopter's landing gear slipped through the towrope, grabbing the wave bike. The wave reached out and tried to grab the helicopter. The copter's blades chopped at its big watery claw.

Whoosh! The helicopter flew away, carrying Didj to safety.

The wave roared angrily. It shook its fist at the helicopter . . . and dropped Swamp into the water at the same time.

Swamp plunged under the water. He stayed calm and reached for the tail strap around his tail. Pulling himself up, he found his board. He climbed up and started to paddle.

Didj had said the Giant Fist would be behind the monster wave. But where was it?

69

Chapter Twelve: Swamp Versus the Giant Fist

Bobbing on the water, he peered into the distance. His eyes widened as an even mightier wave came thundering in. It grew larger and larger as it came closer to Swamp.

"This is it," Swamp said. It was the one. He could feel it in his bones. But how could he catch up to it?

Vrooom! Didj rode up on the wave bike.

"Hook up, Swamp!" he called out. "We got this!"

"Are you sure?" Swamp asked. "That thing is . . . the biggest wave ever."

"That's why nobody talks about it!" Didj shouted over the rushing water.

The enormous wave looked dark and angry. Before his eyes, the wave took the shape of one terrifying Fist. Swamp felt scared for a second, but he pushed it away.

It was an EXTREME wave. But he was an EXTREME wallaby.

"You're not gonna catch me like that other wave!" Swamp yelled. "I'm ready for you!" He steadied himself as the wave swelled up underneath him. In seconds he and Didj matched the speed of the Giant Fist.

There was only one more thing left to do. He was ready to let go of the rope. Every muscle strained as he kept his balance.

He was doing it! He was riding the Giant Fist!

"WHAT A BEAUTY!" he yelled over the wave's giant roar. "This is it! This is incredible! I'm doing it!"

He cut down through the face of the wave, sliding along the surface at high speed. He changed directions over and over. He was carving the water like he always knew he could. A feeling of pure joy washed over him. He didn't want to stop. He wanted to surf the wave forever!

Then the Giant Fist curled its fingers, like a boxer ready to deliver a knockout punch. Swamp looked up and swallowed hard. There was no escape. The wave was going to dump him, hard.

This was going to hurt.

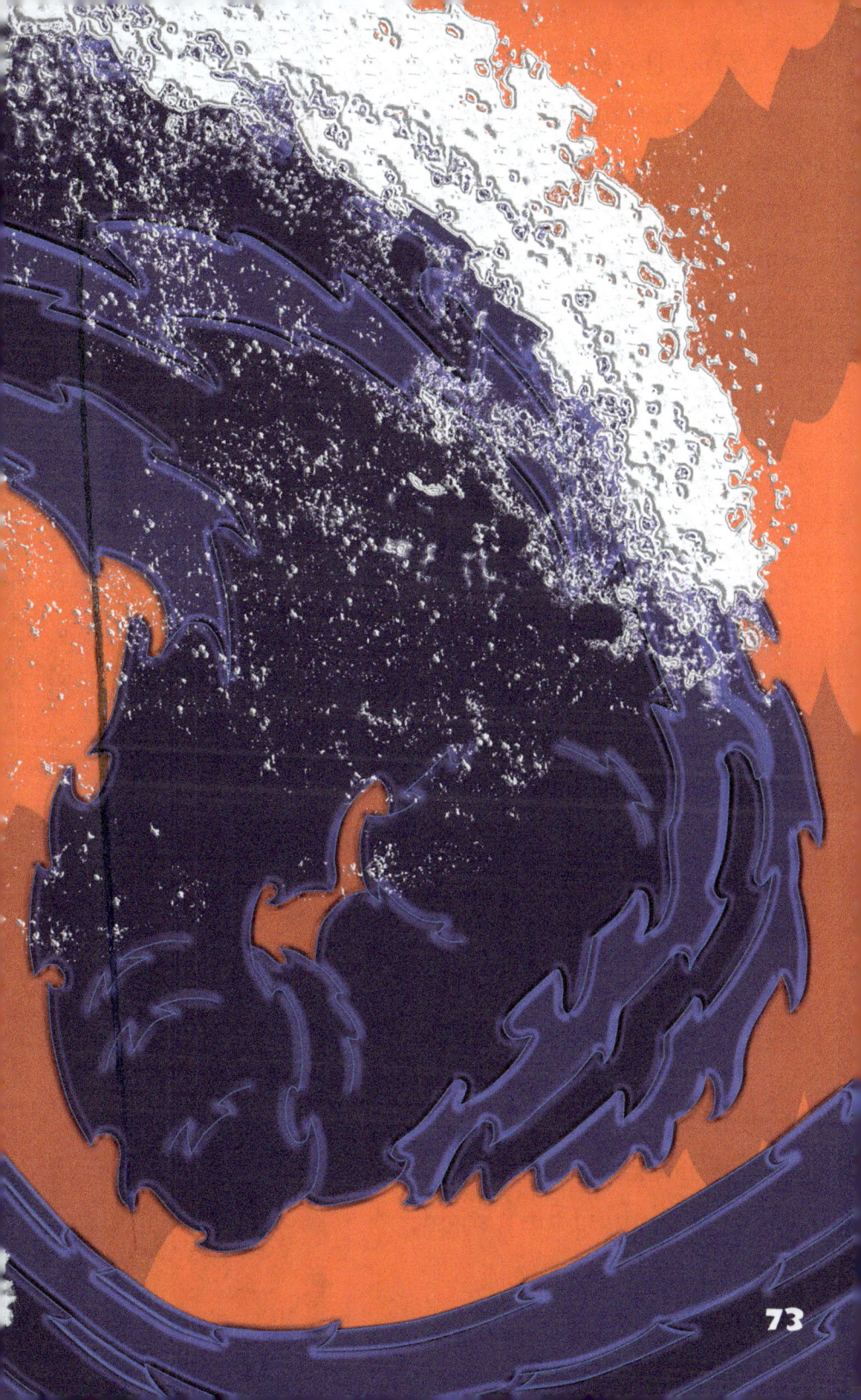

Bam! The Giant Fist dumped Swamp, forcing him under the water. Swamp felt limp as the wave dumped him big time. A mountain of water had crashed over him, he held his breath as tonnes of turbulent water like a giant washing machine kept him trapped inside it's spin cycle. He tumbled again and again within the crashing wave. He didn't know up from down or down from up. His lungs burned as he continued to hold his breath. A current as powerful as a rip carried him away.

On the shore, Swampah, Rocksy, Didj, Bilby, and Jilby all gasped.

"Where is he?" Rocksy asked worriedly.

Then Bilby and Jilby pointed.

"Look! Look!"

Something furry, soggy,

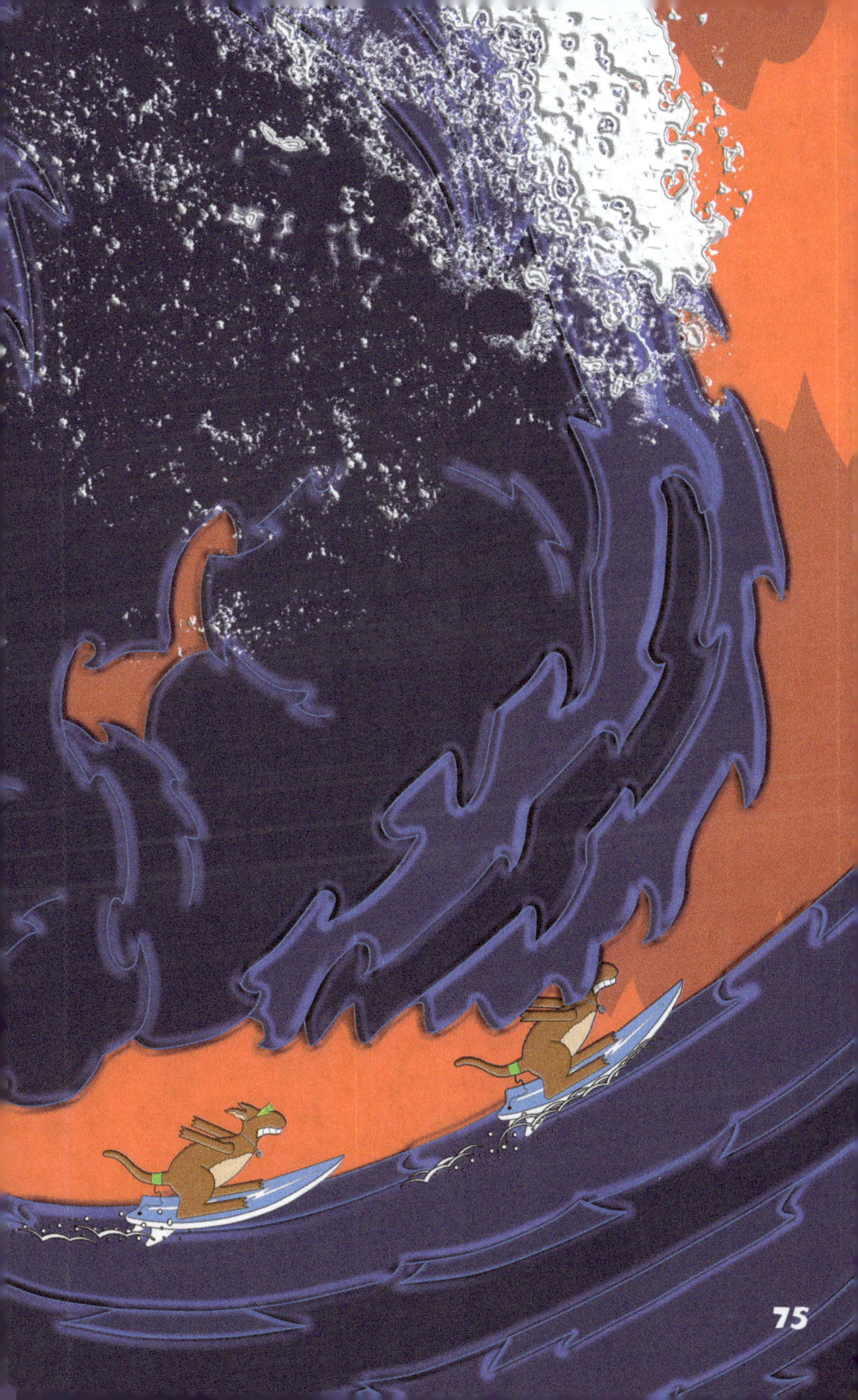

and brown was riding into shore on a small wave.

"It looks like a balled-up wet sock," said Swampah.

"It looks like a bag of rotten potatoes," said Didj.

Rocksy's face lit up. "It's Swamp!"

Swamp waved as the wave carried him in. Everybody clapped and cheered.

Swamp jumped off the board and hopped over to his family and friends. He chest-bumped Didj.

"You did it, Swamp!" he said.

"Yeah, I did," Swamp said.

Rocksy hugged him. "That was pretty EXTREME, Swamp!"

Bilby and Jilby wrapped their arms around his legs.

"Nobody can surf like you, Swamp," said Jilby.

"Yeah, nobody," agreed Bilby.

Swamp looked at Swampah.

"When did you learn how to fly a helicopter?"

Swampah shrugged. "There are a lot of things I can do for an old fella," he said.

The Emu strode up to them.

"Congratulations!" she said. "You have passed the first challenge!"

She slipped a meda
picture of the Giant Fist

over Swamp's head. It had a
on it.

Rocksy. "So what's the next

anded her a flyer.

Congratulations!
You beat the first EXTREME
Outback Challenge.
Now you're ready for Round 2.
Here in rhyme is what you must do.
First, find a super-sized didgeridoo.
And then head over to Kakadu,
where a big crocodile will be waiting for you!

"Cool!" said Didj. "Let's jump in the kombi."

"Wait! There's something I need to do first," said Swamp.

"What's that?" Swampah asked.

Swamp yawned.

"How about a nice warm campfire on the beach and a good night's sleep? I need to rest these wallaby bones."

Some of the CHALLENGE TEAMS

Combat Wombats

Kruising Koalas

The Boomeroos

79